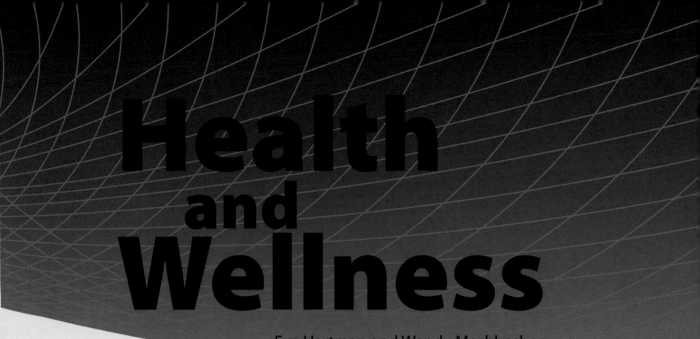

Health
and
Wellness

Eve Hartman and Wendy Meshbesher

www.raintreepublishers.co.uk
Visit our website to find out more information about Raintree books.

To order:
☎ Phone +44 (0) 1865 888066
🖹 Fax +44 (0) 1865 314091
🖥 Visit www.raintreepublishers.co.uk

Raintree is an imprint of Capstone Global Library Limited, a company incorporated in England and Wales having its registered office at 7 Pilgrim Street, London, EC4V 6LB – Registered company number: 6695582

"Raintree" is a registered trademark of Pearson Education Limited, under licence to Capstone Global Library Limited

Edited by Adam Miller, Andrew Farrow, and Adrian Vigliano
Designed by Philippa Jenkins and Ken Vail
Original illustrations © Capstone Global Library Limited 2009
Picture research by Ruth Blair
Originated by Raintree
Printed in and bound by CTPS (China Translation and Printing Services Ltd)

ISBN 978 1 406211 52 8 (hardback)
13 12 11 10 09
10 9 8 7 6 5 4 3 2 1

British Library Cataloguing in Publication Data
Hartman, Eve and Meshbesher, Wendy
Health and wellness. – (Sci-hi)
613-dc22
A full catalogue record for this book is available from the British Library.

Acknowledgements
The author and publishers are grateful to the following for permission to reproduce copyright material: © iStockphoto/Günay Mutlu contents pp. **iii** (contents top); © iStockphoto/Jose Manuel Gelpi Diaz pp. **iii** (contents bottom); © iStockphoto p. **5**; © Blend Images/Alamy p. **4**; © EDELMANN / SCIENCE PHOTO LIBRARY p. **6**; © iStockphoto/Leigh Schindler p. **7**; © iStockphoto/Maciej Bogacz p. **8**; © iStockphoto/ Jose Manuel Gelpi Diaz p. **9**; © iStockphoto/Michael DeLeon p. **9**; © Compassionate Eye Foundation/Sam Diephuis/ Getty p. **10**; © iStockphoto/daniel rodriguez p. **11**; © iStockphoto/Catherine Yeulet p. **13**; © STEPHANIE SCHULLER / SCIENCE PHOTO LIBRARY p. **15** (top); © CONEYL JAY / SCIENCE PHOTO LIBRARY p. **15** (bottom); © BIOLOGY MEDIA / SCIENCE PHOTO LIBRARY p. **17**; © iStockphoto/cecilie johanse p. **16** (left); © Science Photo Library p. **16** (right); © WILL & DENI MCINTYRE/SCIENCE PHOTO LIBRARY p. **18**; © SAMUEL ASHFIELD/SCIENCE PHOTO LIBRARY p. **19**; © SHEILA TERRY/SCIENCE PHOTO LIBRARY p. **21**; © Andrew Twort/Alamy p. **23**; © David J. Green - Lifestyle / Alamy p. **24**; © UpperCut Images / Alamy p. **27**; © iStockphoto/Graça Victoria p. **29**; © iStockphoto/ Aleksey Puris p. **28**; © iStockphoto/Thomas Shortell p. **30**; © iStockphoto/Günay Mutlu p. **31**; © HEALTH PROTECTION AGENCY / SCIENCE PHOTO LIBRARY p. **32**; © superclic / Alamy p. **34**; © JIM VARNEY / SCIENCE PHOTO LIBRARY p. **35**; © PR. M. BRAUNER / SCIENCE PHOTO LIBRARY p. **37**; © Science Photo Library p. **37**; © JUPITERIMAGES/ Thinkstock / Alamy p. **39**; © Bubbles Photolibrary / Alamy p. **41**; © Shutterstock background images and design features.

Cover photograph of a teenage girl reproduced with permission of © Punchstock/Photographers Choice **main**; cover photograph of medicine tablets reproduced with permission of © Alamy/B.A.E. Inc. **inset**.

The publishers would like to thank literacy consultant Nancy Harris and content consultant Ann Fullick for their assistance in the preparation of this book.

Contents

Why do dentists take X-rays of your teeth? Find out on page 31!

How tall would this infant be as an adult if she kept growing at the same speed that she's growing now?

Turn to page 9 to find out!

Some words are shown in bold, **like this**. These words are explained in the glossary. You will find important information and definitions underlined, <u>like this</u>.

HEALTH AND WELLNESS

What is the most complicated and powerful object that you use every day? The answer is your body. The human body is made of more parts than a typical machine, and it does more tasks than any computer.

Yet like a machine, the human body needs to be used and cared for properly. <u>Taking care of your body is one of the keys to a long, healthy life.</u> This book will present many facts about the human body and the best ways to care for it.

What is the human body?

The human body is an example of an **organism**. An organism is an individual living thing. Like other organisms, the body is made of tiny units called **cells**. It has maybe ten trillion cells. Ten trillion is a 1 with 13 zeros after it!

The body's cells are highly organized. Similar cells join together to form **tissues**. A variety of tissues make up a body part called an **organ**. The heart and liver are examples of organs. Organs across the body may work together as **organ systems**.

We know more about the way our bodies work now than ever before. But new discoveries are still being made!

TASKS FOR ORGAN SYSTEMS

Every organ system performs a specific task. The **circulatory system**, for example, includes the heart, blood vessels, and blood. Blood vessels carry blood through the body as it circulates (moves through the body on a closed path). The circulatory system brings food and oxygen to all body cells, and it removes wastes. The **nervous system** includes the brain, spinal cord, and nerves. In the nervous system, the spinal cord and nerves carry messages to and from the brain. The brain then controls other organ systems.

The body's organ systems work together to maintain all body functions. In a healthy body, every organ system works at its best.

When exercising, the circulatory system kicks into high gear. The system rushes extra blood (which contains oxygen and nutrients) to the parts of the body that are working the hardest. The circulatory system even helps regulate body temperature!

The early years

Although every human life is unique in many ways, all humans share many of the same experiences. <u>Humans pass through characteristic stages of growth and development.</u> Before birth are the stages of pregnancy, during which the body develops from a single **cell**. Infancy and childhood are the first stages after birth.

A healthy diet, exercise, and avoiding alcohol and tobacco all help a pregnant woman to give birth to a healthy baby.

Early pregnancy

A woman who is carrying a developing baby is described as pregnant. A pregnancy typically lasts about 9 months.

The first cell of a new human forms when a male reproductive cell (sperm cell) joins a female reproductive cell (egg cell). The new cell quickly begins dividing. It forms two cells, then four cells, then eight cells, and so on.

The growing mass of cells is called an **embryo**. After about a week, the embryo attaches to the wall of the **uterus**. The uterus is a chamber in the female reproductive system.

From foetus to baby

The body's shape begins to appear during the embryo stage. Early forms of the spine and brain also begin to form. <u>At about 8 weeks, the embryo becomes a **foetus**. This is when **organs** and **organ systems** develop.</u> Many organs begin working.

When a baby is born, the lungs breathe air for the first time. Quickly the baby uses the mouth and digestive tract, typically by taking milk from the mother.

A HEALTHY PREGNANCY

During a pregnancy, the developing baby depends completely on the mother. If the mother practises healthy habits, it is likely that the baby will be healthy, too.

A pregnant woman should avoid alcohol, tobacco products, and certain drugs and medicines. Each can pass from the mother's blood supply to the baby's blood, where it can cause much damage.

Infancy

Compared to many baby animals, a newborn human is especially weak and helpless. A newborn can move arms and legs, but cannot crawl or walk. The newborn also needs liquid food, which ideally is milk from the mother.

The infancy stage lasts from birth until about the age of one. <u>An infant changes greatly during the first year, more so than during any year that follows.</u> The infant grows about 25 centimetres (10 inches) and triples in weight. Bones harden and muscles develop. The brain learns how to use these muscles to move the body. The infant also learns to recognize new words and faces.

As an infant changes into an older baby, both the infant and caregivers face many challenges. Gradually the baby learns to communicate with words, eat solid food, and use the toilet.

Childhood

Very young children are called toddlers because of their unsteady walk. The hips and legs have not yet fully developed.

<u>The bodies of children grow and develop every year.</u> Children also learn new knowledge and skills, and they forge friendships and family relationships. Although children learn to take care of themselves in many ways, they still depend on their parents or guardians.

With each passing year, an infant or child learns new skills and develops more independence. The first year brings the greatest changes to the body.

BABY TEETH

Most organs grow gradually during childhood to take on their adult sizes. Teeth are a big exception. Baby teeth develop early and help with chewing and speaking. They also hold space in the jaw for permanent teeth. Beginning at about the age of six, permanent teeth push out the baby teeth above or below them. Permanent teeth are meant to stay in place for life!

SPEED GROWTH

Human bodies develop at an incredible rate during their first year. If a typical infant kept growing at the first year growth rate, that person would reach adulthood with a height of about 5 metres (16 feet)!

Adolescence and adulthood

As children approach their teenage years, their bodies begin to change in new ways. This stage of life is called **adolescence**. <u>During adolescence, the body develops new male or female **traits**.</u> These traits include further development of the reproductive system.

Puberty and adolescence

The time that adolescence begins is called **puberty**. Most girls reach puberty between the ages of 9 and 13. Most boys reach it two years after the girls do. In both genders, however, puberty may be entered a little before or after the typical range.

<u>Puberty occurs because of changes in the levels of **oestrogen** or **testosterone**.</u> **Hormones** are substances that cause **cells** to develop in certain ways. Oestrogen is the hormone in girls. It comes from the ovaries, which are the female reproductive organs that produce eggs. Testosterone is the hormone in boys. It comes from the testes, which are the male reproductive glands that produce sperm. Both hormones **stimulate** reproductive organs to develop. Oestrogen also triggers the onset of the **menstrual cycle**, also known as a period. This is the monthly cycle of the female reproductive system.

At the age of 10, many girls have entered puberty while boys have not. The girl in this picture has begun to grow towards her adult height. The boy will probably have to wait a few years to begin his growth spurt.

More changes

<u>Oestrogen and testosterone also stimulate secondary sexual characteristics.</u> These are traits apart from the reproductive organs but still specific to gender. Female traits include breasts and wide hips. Male traits include facial hair and a deep voice.

Other changes of adolescence include the growth of body hair under the arms and in the pelvic region. The body also grows significantly taller, an event called a **growth spurt**. By the end of adolescence, the body has reached its adult height.

By the age of 18, boys and girls have nearly completed adolescence. Their bodies have acquired male or female adult traits. By this time, boys have had their chance to go through a growth spurt, too.

Changing minds

Adolescence also brings changes to the mind. Many adolescents feel self-conscious or embarrassed about the changes to their bodies. Mood swings are common during this stage, as are a variety of feelings about the opposite gender.

Adolescents often are tempted by risky actions and behaviours. Yet many begin to look at their lives in more mature and abstract ways. They may make serious plans for their lives as adults.

Adults

Adulthood is the mature stage of human life, meaning that all body systems are fully developed. For much of adulthood, the body may change very little from year to year.

As the adult body ages, however, body systems gradually slow down and use less energy. Adults who continue eating habits from their teenage years are prone to weight gain, especially if they do not exercise sufficiently. In many sports, athletes typically pass their peak abilities in their twenties or thirties.

As an adult woman ages, she will eventually reach menopause, which is the time when the menstrual cycle stops. Menopause often occurs between the ages of 45 and 55. After menopause, a woman is not able to become pregnant.

Senior adults

By the 60th year, the body has slowed greatly and has changed in many ways. Hair has turned grey, eyesight has become poorer, and wrinkles line the face. The body is also more prone to injury and disease. Nevertheless, the minds of senior adults can be as sharp as ever. With a healthy mind, people can lead active lives at any age.

SENIOR ATHLETES

As well as having sharp minds, many senior adults continue to enjoy athletic lifestyles well past their sixties. New improvements in medical science help make it possible for people to stay healthy and active further into their lives. Every year senior athletes in the United States can enter to compete in the National Senior Olympics. There are 25 events – everything from swimming to basketball to triathlon! The Senior Olympics began in 1987 and has now grown to have over 10,000 competitors. In 2007 the oldest athletes at the games were over 100 years old!

LIFE EXPECTANCY

One hundred years ago, people often died before the age of 50. Today, the average person in the United Kingdom lives to about the age of 79. Improved sanitation and health care are the major reasons why people now lead longer lives.

The oldest known human life lasted 122 years. Scientists have evidence that the body cannot last for much longer than this. <u>Eventually, body cells lose the ability to reproduce. Without new cells to replace the old, body systems weaken and fail.</u>

Body systems slow as adults age, but senior adults can lead active, healthy lives for many years.

Diseases

A disease is a condition that affects the ability of the body to function properly. <u>A wide variety of diseases can affect the body, and the body has many defences against them.</u> These defences are the reason why people stay healthy most of the time, and why they recover after many diseases strike.

Blame the germs!

For most of human history, people had vague or incorrect ideas about the causes of diseases. This began to change when microscopes were invented. By the 19th century, scientists had established that germs cause many diseases. <u>Germs are microscopic living things or particles that can invade the body.</u>

Bacteria, fungi, and protists are examples of germs that are alive. Viruses are germs made of genetic material. Genetic material stores the information of a life form and is passed from parents to their offspring. Viruses trick body **cells** into reproducing virus particles.

SURROUNDED BY GERMS

No matter how hard we try, we humans can't get rid of germs. They swarm over most of the objects we touch every day. Door handles, keyboards, the bottoms of bags and shoes, and toilet seats have some of the highest numbers of germs. But you'll never guess the germiest of all: mobile phones!

Infectious diseases

Germs cause **infectious diseases** (diseases that can be caught). Some infectious diseases are mild, such as colds and athlete's foot. Others are more serious. AIDS is caused by a virus, as is a liver disease called hepatitis.

Germs can spread through air, water, and food. Many germs spread through close contact with an infected person or animal.

Stopping the spread

Washing with soapy water helps kill many types of germs and stops them from spreading. Covering your mouth when you cough or sneeze also stops the spread of germs.

Keeping kitchen surfaces and equipment clean helps stop food-borne germs. Many foods need to be kept cool or frozen to keep germs from growing on them.

Bacteria live almost everywhere! These colonies of bacteria grew on an ordinary human hand. The light-coloured areas on the hand show the largest colonies of bacteria.

Three lines of defence

The body has three lines of defence to fight invading germs. <u>When one line of defence fails against germs, the next line is called into action.</u> These defences keep you healthy and help you recover from disease.

1

First line

The body's barriers to its environment are the first line of defence. These barriers include skin, tears, mucus in the nose and throat, and acid in the stomach. Most germs cannot pass these barriers alive.

2

Second line

Parts of the blood act as the second line of defence. If germs invade through a cut or scrape, for example, types of white blood cells will try to destroy them. A rise in body temperature, called a fever, helps slow the growth of germs.

VACCINES

Diseases such as polio and smallpox were once common and deadly. Today, the use of vaccines has all but eliminated them.

Vaccines work by preparing the immune system to fight a specific kind of germ. Most vaccines are made from weakened or killed forms of a germ. When the immune system meets the vaccine, it makes antibodies against it. Then, should the real germ invade, the immune system is ready to fight it.

3

Third line

Special types of white blood cells make up the third line of defence, which is also called the **immune system**. The immune system makes **antibodies** in the blood. The antibodies recognize specific germs, and the immune system then attacks and destroys the germs.

When a new kind of germ invades the body, the immune system needs time to make an antibody against it. But then it "remembers" that antibody. A type of germ may cause an illness once, but not if it tries to invade a second time.

Non-infectious diseases

Non-infectious diseases do not spread from person to person, nor do germs cause them. These diseases have a variety of causes.

Some non-infectious diseases strike when body parts wear out. Arthritis, for example, is caused by worn-out joints, making movement painful.

A poor diet can lead to many diseases. The body needs many vitamins and minerals, and lack of any of them can lead to serious illness. Overeating can lead to disease, too.

Genes carry information for development and are passed down from parents. Diseases may also be inherited through genes. An example is sickle cell disease, in which small blood vessels are blocked by crescent-shaped red blood cells. Red-green colour blindness and haemophilia, in which the blood clots poorly or not at all, are also inherited diseases.

Cancer

Cancer is a general term for a variety of non-infectious diseases that strike across the body. In a cancer, abnormally-shaped cells grow and divide rapidly. Typically these cells form a mass or lump called a **tumour**. If left untreated, cancer cells can spread to many body parts.

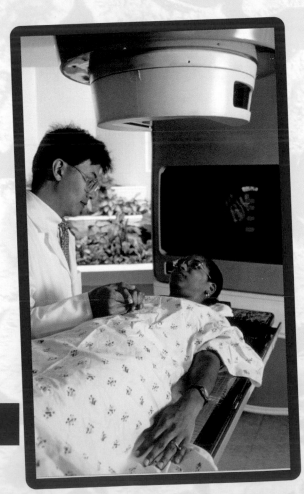

Cancer often strikes randomly. Yet certain behaviours make cancer more likely. Smoking tobacco products can lead to lung cancer. High-intensity sunlight can lead to skin cancer.

Many forms of cancer once were deadly. Now more cancers than ever before can be detected early and treated, and even cured.

Diabetes

<u>With diabetes, the body does not make or use insulin properly.</u> Insulin is a hormone that moves **glucose** (sugar) out of the blood into the cells where it is needed. Excess blood glucose can damage the eyes, kidneys, and other organs.

Diabetes cannot be cured, but it can be managed.

Disease report

- What diseases are affecting people today?
- What parts of the world are most at risk from West Nile virus and malaria?
- How can we solve deadly problems like **antibiotic** resistance and hospital infection?

Search newspapers, magazines, and the Internet to find answers to these and other questions that interest you.

Diabetes patients need to monitor their glucose levels carefully. This girl needs to take shots of insulin. This helps to regulate glucose levels in her blood.

Diet and nutrition

Nutrients are materials in food that the body needs and uses. Your body needs a variety of nutrients, and no single food contains all of them. <u>A wide variety of foods can supply the body with all the nutrients it needs.</u> With the right combination of foods, the body can work at its best.

Many nutrients

Your digestive system breaks down food into tiny pieces. Although the foods you eat may have many tastes and textures, they mostly contain only a few types of nutrients.

Carbohydrates

Sugars and starches are types of carbohydrates. Each carbohydrate is broken down into **glucose**, the **molecule** that the body uses for energy. A molecule is a tiny group of atoms. **Calories** are the units used to measure the energy in food. Most calories in the diet come from carbohydrates.

Proteins

The digestive system breaks down proteins, which are **organic compounds**, (compounds that come from living things) into the **amino acids** they are made of. Amino acids are molecules that are critical to life and play a role in metabolism (body processes that work to use food and nutrients). **Cells** reassemble the amino acids into new proteins that they can use. Cells need proteins for growth and repair.

Lipids

Oils and fats are made of molecules called lipids. The body needs only certain lipids and in limited amounts, as they are very high in calories. Vegetable oils are a healthier source of lipids than are animal fats. Lipids are needed in order for the body to absorb certain vitamins.

Vitamins and minerals

The body needs both vitamins and minerals in relatively small amounts. Vitamins help the body perform certain **chemical reactions**, such as regulating cell growth. Minerals help make up healthy cells and body fluids.

Water

The body is mostly water, and it is essential to replace the water your body loses. You can get the water you need either from drinking fluids or from eating watery foods.

Vitamins, minerals, and other nutrients are put into pills or powders. **Nutritionists** sometimes recommend these products to aid, but not replace, a balanced diet.

VITAMINS AND MINERALS

What foods do you eat on a regular basis? Are you getting lots of one kind of vitamin or mineral and not much of another? Have a look at this table to learn more.

Vitamin or mineral	Sources	Purpose
Vitamin A	liver, carrots, broccoli, leafy vegetables	for healthy eyes and skin
B vitamins (such as B_1, B_2, B_3, B_9, B_{12})	potatoes, bananas, many meat and fish products	support the nervous system, **immune system**, cell growth, and many body functions
Vitamin C	citrus fruits	helps make collagen, a part of skin, gums, and other tissues
Vitamin D	fish, fortified milk, and other products	for healthy bones
Iron	meat, beans, leafy vegetables	for healthy red blood cells
Calcium	milk and dairy products	for healthy bones and teeth

A balanced diet

To help people choose the variety of foods they need, dieticians (experts in diet and nutrition) organize foods into five food groups. <u>A balanced diet includes foods from each food group.</u> Together, the food groups provide all of the nutrients the body needs.

Bread, rice, potatoes, pasta

Bread, rice, potatoes, and pasta supply carbohydrates, the source of energy for the body. Some experts argue that foods from this group should be kept to a minimum in the diet. According to their reasoning, high levels of body fat and **cholesterol** come from excess carbohydrate in the diet, not excess fat. Cholesterol is a natural compound that is found in most body tissues. But some forms of cholesterol may harden arteries (a condition in which arteries are blocked with fatty deposits).

Meat, fish, eggs, and beans

These foods are rich in proteins. Many people choose not to eat meat or other animal products. They need to take in proteins from other sources, such as beans and nuts.

Fruits and vegetables

Fruits provide many vitamins and minerals not always found in other groups. Oranges, grapefruit, and other citrus fruits, for example, provide vitamin C. Fruits also provide **dietary fibre**, which is material that helps food move through the digestive tract.

Like fruits, vegetables also provide vitamins, minerals, and dietary fibre. Leafy vegetables are rich in iron, a mineral needed for healthy blood. Carrots contain a nutrient that the body converts to vitamin A, important for healthy eyesight.

Milk and dairy foods

This group includes milk, cheese, and yoghurt. These foods are rich in calcium, an important mineral for healthy bones and teeth.

Foods high in fat and sugar

Foods high in fat and sugar, such as cakes and biscuits, should make up only a small part of your diet.

Vegetables are very diverse. Each contains nutrients that help a plant survive, and in turn can help people, too.

LACTOSE INTOLERANCE

The sugar in milk is called **lactose**. Many people do not digest lactose well, and are described as lactose intolerant. Many such people can gain the benefits of milk from fermented milk products, which include cheese and yoghurt.

Diet challenges

Maintaining a balanced diet depends on eating three healthy meals a day, including breakfast, lunch, and dinner. Eating is also a social event, and should be enjoyed with friends or family.

For many people, maintaining body weight is one of the biggest challenges for their diet. Today, more Britons are seriously overweight than ever before. Nutritionists point to many possible causes of this problem, including poor dietary choices, lack of exercise, and the typically poor nutritional content of many processed foods. These foods are sometimes high in fat, salt, or sugar, and low in vitamins and other nutrients.

Teenagers often are concerned about their body weight. Many try fad diets or other schemes to lose weight. Others eat a very poor diet and suffer from low body weight. These kinds of behaviours are not healthy.

Films, magazines, and television programmes often show "perfect people", whose body shapes are impossible to maintain in good health. Some fashion models have suffered from poor health because of their efforts to remain extremely thin.

Dieticians and nutritionists

If you have questions about your diet or body weight, you can ask a dietician or nutritionist. These health experts work with people to find the diet that is right for them.

<u>A dietician will tell you that body weight cannot be safely gained or lost significantly over just a few days or weeks.</u> Rather, the key is to combine a healthy, balanced diet with daily exercise and a positive outlook.

Healthy choices?

In the United States, fast food accounts for about half of all money made from restaurants. It is also gaining in popularity in other parts of the world, such as Asia and the Middle East. The fast food industry in India is growing by around 40 per cent a year!

FOOD LABELS

Labels on food packaging list the nutritional value of the food inside them. Compare the labels for five breakfast cereals. Which cereal supplies the most vitamins and minerals? Which supplies sugar and calories you might not need?

Physical fitness

A body that is **physically fit** is strong, durable, and flexible. <u>The key to physical fitness is to exercise for at least 30 minutes a day.</u> Being physically fit also helps people feel better about themselves and sharpens the mind. It even improves sleep!

Aerobic exercise

Scientists classify exercise into two groups. **Aerobic exercise** is performed with moderate intensity over a relatively long period of time. Jogging, cycling, swimming, and football are examples of aerobic exercise.

The term aerobic means "with oxygen". Aerobic exercise helps muscles use oxygen to generate energy efficiently. It also improves the heart and lungs, as well as muscle tone throughout the body.

Anaerobic exercise

In contrast, **anaerobic exercise** is intense and quick. Weightlifting is one example. Anaerobic exercise helps build up muscle mass and strength.

<u>A healthy exercise plan should include both aerobic and anaerobic exercises.</u> Many trainers encourage people to alternate these two types of exercise from day to day, as well as to alternate the muscle groups being exercised.

Useful exercise can be done alone or in a group, or by playing a team sport. You can choose any form of exercise that you enjoy.

The dangers of anabolic steroids

The term "anabolic" refers to the building up of body tissues. Drugs called **anabolic steroids** can build up muscle mass, acting as an artificial substitute for anaerobic exercise. Yet these drugs have many harmful and dangerous side effects. They include reduced fertility, mood swings, and increased likelihood of injury.

The use of anabolic steroids and other drugs does not lead to physical fitness. Any perceived benefit they may bring is far outweighed by their drawbacks.

Keeping healthy

No one likes to be ill. Even a scratchy throat or a mild rash are annoying. <u>Keeping the body clean helps prevent many diseases.</u> The practice of keeping clean is called **hygiene**. Good hygiene helps people look and feel their best.

Preventing acne

Regular washing and bathing are part of good hygiene for people of any age, but are especially important during the teenage years. <u>Washing the face removes sweat and skin oils, thus helping to prevent a disease called **acne**.</u>

Acne is characterized by red or white skin lesions, commonly called spots or pimples. In severe acne, the lesions can become infected and leave small scars.

Preventing body odour

Sweat by itself is odourless. The odour of an unwashed body comes from **bacteria** (single-celled, microscopic **organisms**) that live on the skin and that sweat helps promote. <u>Washing regularly with soap and water helps stop body odour.</u> Also helpful are anti-perspirants, which are chemicals that reduce sweat. They are used under the arms, where sweat often collects.

Anti-perspirants come in different strengths, odours, and styles of application. While useful, they are not a substitute for daily washing.

ACNE

Acne is common during adolescence because of the body's rising levels of sex hormones. Some of these hormones trigger glands in the skin to release more sweat and skin oil. They combine with dead skin cells or other tissues to clog a pore.

Some research suggests that a diet rich in fats and sugars can promote acne. If so, it is yet another reason to avoid "junk food", such as soft drinks, sweets, and extra-sweet cakes and biscuits.

Acne is a common disease of adolescence. Many medications help fight acne. Only in severe cases is a doctor's help required for treatment.

Cavities and gum disease

Food is fuel for the body. Unfortunately, it also is fuel for bacteria. <u>Many kinds of bacteria live in the mouth and can do much damage there.</u> The damage begins when bacteria invade the teeth or gums.

A cavity is a bacterial infection of a tooth. Most cavities are confined to the **enamel**, which is the hard outer layer of a tooth. If the infection grows, however, it may spread into the root of the tooth. Such infections can be quite painful.

An infection of the gums is called **gingivitis**. If it is allowed to continue, it may eat away at the gums until teeth literally fall out.

Oral hygiene

The best way to prevent infection to the teeth and gums is to practise good oral hygiene. Oral hygiene includes brushing teeth after meals, cleaning teeth and gums with dental floss, and gargling with mouthwash. These practices clean the mouth and slow the growth of bacteria.

Dentists are experts on oral hygiene. Seeing a dentist at least twice a year will help you keep a healthy mouth.

Orthodontists are dentists who specialise in fixing the alignment of teeth, often by installing braces. The prefix *ortho-* means "straight".

TWO SETS OF TEETH

Everyone gets two sets of teeth. The first set of 20 teeth is called the baby teeth. Beginning at about the age of six, these teeth are replaced by a set of 32 teeth, called the adult teeth or permanent teeth.

Permanent teeth sometimes do not enter the mouth correctly. Often they are pushed forwards or backwards, or off slightly to one side. Braces on the teeth can help fix this problem.

Dentists take X-rays to find hidden cavities. The dark area shows one.

cavity

Optometrists are experts in the eye. They can correct people's vision by prescribing glasses.

Help from experts

If you feel ill or hurt, ask for help from a parent, teacher, or other trusted adult. Do not ignore sharp pains or expect them to go away on their own. Pain shows that a body part is injured and needs rest and attention. Ignoring pain could lead to a more serious illness or injury.

When symptoms are serious, you may need attention from a doctor or other health care expert. Other members of the health care team include nurses, medical technicians, therapists, and pharmacists.

Nurses are health care professionals who work under the supervision of doctors. Medical technicians are usually trained to perform certain medical tests. Therapists help people recover from injuries and illness. Pharmacists make sure patients get the medicines that doctors recommend.

MEDICAL SPECIALITIES

Most doctors pursue a speciality, meaning they treat only certain types of patients or certain diseases.

Specialist	Treats
Cardiologist	heart disease
Endocrinologist	diseases of glands
Gastroenterologist	the digestive system
Nephrologist	kidney diseases
Ophthalmologist	eyes and vision
Orthopaedist	bone diseases and injuries
Paediatrician	children
Surgeons (many types)	many diseases and injuries through surgical operations

Medicines

A **drug** is any substance that changes how the body functions. A **medicine** is a drug that is intended to improve body functions. Some medicines improve only the symptoms of disease. Aspirin relieves pain, for example, but does not fight the disease or injury that causes the pain.

Other medicines treat the disease itself. **Antibiotics**, for example, kill or damage invading bacteria. Penicillin, erythromycin, and cephalosporins are examples of antibiotics. Some other types of medicine are part of **chemotherapy**, a treatment used to kill cancer cells.

Aspirin and other mild medicines are available for any adult to purchase. They are **over-the-counter** medicines, and are sold at chemists and supermarkets. Stronger medicines, however, are available only from a doctor's order. They are **prescription medicines**, so named because a doctor must prescribe their use.

Alcohol, tobacco, and certain illegal **drugs** each change the way the body functions. A user may find their initial effects to be pleasing. Unfortunately, these substances cause much damage, especially with repeated use. They are **addictive**, meaning they can make the user want more of them. The body might even need more of the substance to maintain itself.

<u>Users of alcohol, tobacco, or drugs can easily become addicted – and find their addictions difficult to break.</u> These addictions have ruined many lives.

Alcohol

Alcohol is a chemical that depresses the **nervous system**. Although beer and wine have a lower percentage of alcohol than spirits, the alcohol in each is the same substance.

<u>The higher the level of alcohol in the blood, the more the nervous system is affected.</u> Even moderate levels of alcohol will slow reaction time, which is why a person should never operate a motor vehicle after drinking alcohol. High levels of alcohol typically cause drastic changes of mood, slurred speech, and impaired ability to think and reason.

Companies that sell alcohol use appealing adverts and packaging to sell their products. Your health and welfare is not their main concern.

Alcoholism

Long-term abuse of alcohol can permanently damage the brain, stomach, liver, and other body **organs**. It also leads to **alcoholism**, a disease that involves both a physical and emotional dependence on alcohol.

Without alcohol, the nervous system of an alcoholic produces shaking, seizures, and hallucinations (false visions). Alcoholics find themselves losing control of their lives, as alcohol becomes more important than their jobs or school, friends, and family.

This teenager is being tested for alcohol with a breathalyzer device. Any person caught driving after drinking alcohol faces severe penalties, including the loss of their driver's licence.

Recovering from alcohol abuse

If you or a family member suffers from alcohol abuse, help is available. Clinics and treatment centres can help people break the hold of alcohol on their lives. An organization called Alateen (see page 47) can help teenagers cope with family members who abuse alcohol.

Tobacco: it's not "cool"

Many people once thought that smoking was a stylish, clever habit. Yet scientific studies have shown that using tobacco products is risky and dangerous – not "cool" at all.

Tobacco products include cigarettes, cigars, and chewing tobacco. Each type contains **nicotine**, a drug that **stimulates** (excites) the nervous system. It is also highly addictive, especially among teenagers. <u>Teenagers who begin a tobacco habit often develop a lifelong addiction.</u>

Harm from tobacco

The burning of tobacco produces more than 4,000 chemicals, many of which are harmful. Tobacco smoke also creates a thick, sticky substance called tar. Tar builds up in a smoker's lungs, where it often leads to a thick voice and a hacking cough. Smoking causes diseases such as emphysema, which brings shortness of breath as the lungs become less elastic, and lung cancer.

Tobacco use can also damage the heart and **circulatory system**, as it leads to the hardening of arteries. It can damage the mouth, teeth, and bones, and even discolour the skin. Smokers often appear pale and in ill health. They are poor athletes, too.

Tobacco warnings worldwide

SMOKING CAUSES MOUTH AND THROAT CANCER
Australia

SMOKING SEVERELY HARMS YOU AND THE PEOPLE AROUND YOU
Austria and Germany

SMOKING CAUSES HEART DISEASE
Russia

SMOKING CAUSES AGEING OF THE SKIN
Ireland

SMOKING DURING PREGNANCY HARMS YOUR CHILD'S HEALTH
France

WARNING: CIGARETTES CAN CAUSE LUNG CANCER
85% of lung cancers are caused by smoking
80% of lung cancer victims die within three years
Canada

SMOKELESS TOBACCO

Smokeless tobacco includes products called snuff and chewing tobacco. They are designed to be chewed or sucked. The user spits out the dark, tobacco-stained saliva that accumulates.

Unfortunately, smokeless tobacco is just as harmful as cigarettes and cigars. Long-time users may lose their teeth, gums, and even large parts of their faces to cancerous tumours.

SECOND-HAND SMOKE

You can suffer the bad effects of tobacco just from being near where it is used. **Second-hand smoke** enters the air from a burning cigarette or cigar, or from the mouth of a smoker. This smoke contains a huge number of chemicals, many of which are poisonous or cause cancer. Lawmakers cite the dangers of second-hand smoke for the banning of smoking in restaurants, offices, and other public places.

normal, healthy lungs

lungs of a tobacco smoker

Tobacco products contain poisons that damage the lungs and other organs.

Drug abuse

Any drug can be abused, meaning used improperly so it harms the body. <u>For especially dangerous drugs, even a single dose can cause great damage.</u> Moreover, many drugs are very addictive.

MARIJUANA

Marijuana comes from the cannabis plant. Its active ingredient passes into the brain and affects thought, sensory perception (how the senses experience things), and other functions.

Long-term use of marijuana may cause emotional and physical changes. Yet perhaps its greatest danger is as a "gateway drug", meaning the user feels encouraged to try more serious and harmful drugs.

COCAINE

Cocaine is a stimulant of the nervous system. This means that it makes nerves especially active. For a short while, the user may feel very energetic, restless, and powerful. Yet not long after, the user feels uncomfortable and depressed – and is craving the drug again.

With repeated use, cocaine can cause heart disease and mental illness. Cocaine has caused many deaths.

BARBITURATES

These drugs depress (lessen) the activity of the nervous system. They once were popular treatments for anxiety and sleep disorders. But repeated use will lead to physical tolerance and addiction.

OPIATES

These drugs include morphine and heroin. Morphine is a pain-killing drug often prescribed to surgical patients. Heroin has no medical use and is illegal. All opiates are very addictive and can damage the nervous system with repeated use. They can also cause heart failure and death.

OTHER DRUGS

Even a medicine that a doctor prescribes can cause damage if it is used improperly. Pain killers, diet drugs, and doctor-approved steroids can each be abused, often when patients share their medications with others.

Even a single dose of cocaine, heroin, or other dangerous drugs can be fatal.

Emotional health

The mind and body are connected, and each affects the other. <u>A healthy mind is just as important as a healthy body.</u> Just as good habits can help keep your body healthy, they can help you stay emotionally healthy, too.

Stress

Stress is a part of everyone's life. Examples include the feeling of pressure before a test or performance, changing schools, or losing a close friend or family member.

Yet sometimes stress can be severe and long-lasting. Stress that continues without relief can make it difficult to accomplish goals, and it can damage many body systems.

Activities that relieve stress focus the mind on something new or help it relax. Listening to music, reading a book, writing in a diary, or doing any form of physical exercise are all good activities to try.

DEPRESSION

Everyone feels sad sometimes. Depression is a feeling of sadness or hopelessness that does not leave on its own. Signs of depression include lack of interest in daily life, withdrawal from friends and family, and changes in eating or sleeping habits.

Depression can lead to suicide – one of the main causes of death among teenagers. Fortunately, depression can be treated and cured. A doctor, school counsellor, or another trusted adult can help answer your questions about depression or any emotional health issue.

A good friend or trusted adult can act as a mediator to help resolve a conflict.

Conflict resolution

Teenagers may have conflicts with parents, teachers, classmates, and even good friends. Conflicts may be resolved in many ways, but violence is not one of them. Violence always causes more problems than it solves.

A better choice is to talk about a conflict. Sometimes a **mediator** can help. A mediator is someone who has no stake in the conflict, but helps both sides find an agreement.

Summary

- Proper care for the human body includes keeping clean, eating a healthy diet, daily exercise, and avoiding dangerous drugs and other substances.

- The human body progresses through the stages of infancy, childhood, adolescence, and adulthood. Each stage brings specific changes and challenges.

   Germs cause infectious diseases, meaning diseases that can be caught. Non-infectious diseases (ones that cannot be caught) include arthritis, diabetes, cancer, and inherited diseases.

- Good hygiene helps stop the spread of germs, while medicines and medical treatments can help the body fight diseases.

- A balanced diet provides the wide variety of nutrients that the body needs.

- Alcohol, tobacco, and many illegal drugs are addictive, meaning the body comes to depend on them. Teenagers are especially prone to these addictions.

Quiz

1 During which year of life does the body change the most?

   a. age 0 to 1
   b. age 5 to 6
   c. age 12 to 13
   d. age 24 to 25

2 What causes an infectious disease?

   a. germs
   b. inherited genes
   c. a poor diet
   d. worn-out body parts

3 Breads, cereals, and pasta are good sources of ___.

   a. protein
   b. fats and oils
   c. carbohydrates
   d. calcium and other minerals

4 A healthy exercise plan should include which types of exercise?

   a. aerobic only
   b. anaerobic only
   c. aerobic and anaerobic
   d. team sports only

5 Tobacco contains _____, an addictive drug that stimulates the nervous system.

   a. alcohol
   b. amphetamines
   c. nicotine
   d. tar

6 Which kind of drugs or medicines can be abused?

   a. opiates and barbiturates only
   b. illegal drugs only
   c. prescription medicines only
   d. any type of drug or medicine

Find the answers on page 47.

Glossary

acne skin lesions, or pimples

addictive promoting the desire or need for further use of a substance or activity

adolescence stage of human development during which the body develops many characteristic male or female traits

aerobic exercise physical exercise that helps muscles use oxygen to release energy

alcoholism disease that involves physical and emotional dependence on alcohol

amino acid molecules that are critical to life and play a role in metabolism

anabolic steroids drugs that artificially build up muscles, but with dangerous side effects

anaerobic exercise intense exercise that helps build up muscle mass

antibiotic medicine that slows the growth of, or destroys, micro-organisms such as bacteria

antibody blood protein produced by the body in response to invading micro-organisms or foreign substances in the body

bacteria large group of single-celled, microscopic organisms

calorie unit used to measure the energy in food

cell tiny, basic unit of life, present in all living things

chemical reaction natural reactions in the body, which happen in order to complete tasks

chemotherapy treatment used to kill cancer cells

cholesterol natural compound found in most body tissues. Some forms of cholesterol are thought to be harmful in larger amounts.

circulatory system body system responsible for circulating blood throughout the body. The system includes the heart, blood vessels, and blood.

depression long-lasting feeling of sadness or hopelessness

dietary fibre material in food that moves through the digestive tract and is not taken in by the body

drug any substance that changes how the body functions

embryo for humans, a growing mass of cells that will develop into a foetus

enamel hard outer layer of a tooth

foetus stage of a developing baby from about 8 weeks until birth

gene unit of inheritance that controls or helps control a specific trait

gingivitis infection of the gums

glucose simple type of sugar

growth spurt rapid growth of the body during adolescence

hormone substance that travels through the blood and acts like a chemical messenger from one organ to another

hygiene set of practices that keep the body clean and promote health

immune system specialized white blood cells that recognize and attack germs. It is also called the third line of defence.

infectious disease disease caused by a germ or similar agent, and may be transferred from person to person

lactose the sugar in milk

mediator someone who is not involved in, or has no stake in, a conflict, and who works to help both sides find a solution

medicine drug intended to improve body functions

menopause time in a woman's life when the menstrual cycle stops

menstrual cycle monthly cycle of the female reproductive system; also called a period

molecule tiny group of atoms

nervous system body system that includes the brain, spinal cord, and nerves

nicotine addictive drug in tobacco that stimulates the nervous system

non-infectious disease disease that is not caused by germs and does not spread from person to person

nutrient material in food that the body needs and uses

nutritionist person who studies or is an expert in nutrition

oestrogen hormone that triggers the development of characteristic female traits

organ functional unit of the body that is made from a variety of tissues. The heart, liver, and skin are examples.

organ system group of organs in the body that work together to accomplish a specific task, such as digesting food or circulating blood

organic compound chemical compound that contains carbon, and often is made or used by living things

organism individual living thing

over-the-counter describing medicines that adults can purchase without a doctor's prescription

physical fitness condition in which the body is strong, durable, and flexible

prescription medicine strong medicine that a doctor must prescribe for a patient

puberty time that adolescence begins

second-hand smoke smoke that enters the air from the use of a tobacco product

stimulate to excite, often referring to the body or the nervous system

testosterone hormone that triggers the development of characteristic male traits

tissue group of similar body cells that work together as a unit

trait physical or personality feature. Height and eye colour are two physical human traits. Being shy or confident are personality traits.

tumour growth of body tissue that is not normal. Tumours are sometimes caused by cancer.

uterus chamber in the female reproductive system in which a developing baby grows and matures

vaccine treatment that prepares the immune system for reacting to a specific germ

Find out more

Books

Ingredients of a Balanced Diet (series), Rachel Eugster
  (Franklin Watts, 2007)
Making Healthy Food Choices: Food For Feeling Healthy, Carol Ballard
  (Heinemann Library, 2006)
Teen Issues: Fitness, Joanna Kedge and Joanna Watson
  (Raintree, 2005)

Websites

http://kidshealth.org/
This is an online encyclopedia devoted to health and the human body, with separate sections for kids, teenagers, and adults.

http://www.childrenfirst.nhs.uk/teens/index.html
This website is specially for teenagers and gives advice on all aspects of teenage life.

http://www.london.gov.uk/young-london/kids/issue-zone/ get-healthy/index.jsp
This site offers advice on health including stress and eating the right foods.

http://www.bbc.co.uk/schools/ks3bitesize/science/biology/ health_intro.shtml
You can find out more about health and disease on this website.

http://www.eatwell.gov.uk/healthydiet/nutritionessentials
Find out all you need to know about nutrition.

Organizations

- The British Heart Foundation promotes cardiac health and fitness through programmes, education, and research.

British Heart Foundation
Greater London House
180 Hampstead Road
London
NW1 7AW

Tel: 0300 330 3311
http://www.bhf.org.uk

- Al-Anon, and its affiliate for teenagers called Alateen, help people cope with a family member who abuses alcohol. They sponsor meetings in many communities.

Al-Anon and Alateen
61 Great Dover Street
London
SE1 4YF
United Kingdom

Tel: 020 7403 0888
http://www.al-anonuk.org.uk

Al-Anon and Alateen
Al-Anon Family Groups AGSO
GPO Box 1002
Melbourne VIC 3001
Australia

Tel: 03 9620 2166
http://www.al-anon.alateen.org/australia/alateen.html

Quiz answers

1. a **2.** a **3.** c **4.** c **5.** c **6.** d

Index